English Code 3

Phonics Book

International Phonetic Alphabet (IPA)

IPA SYMBOLS

Consonants

/b/	bag, bike
/d/	desk, opened
/f/	face, free, laugh, photo
/g/	game, good
/h/	hit, hot
/k/	key, kite
/l/	lamp, lucky
/m/	man, monkey
/n/	neck, nut
/ŋ/	ring, flying
/p/	pen, pink
/r/	run, rock
/s/	sun, sell, cycle, grapes
/ʃ/	shirt, shut, shell
/t/	tent, knocked
/θ/	thick, thirsty
/ð/	this, there
/v/	visit, give
/w/	wall, window, what
/ks/	relax, taxi
/j/	yellow, young
/z/	zoo, bananas
/tʃ/	chair, cheese, cheap
/dʒ/	jeans, juice, judge, ginger

Two-Letter Consonant Blend

/bl/	blanket, blue
/pl/	plane, planet
/kl/	clean, climb
/gl/	glass, glove
/fl/	fly, floor
/sl/	sleep, slow
/br/	break, branch
/pr/	price, practice
/kr/	crab
/fr/	fruit
/gr/	grass
/dr/	draw
/tr/	train
/ŋk/	bank, think
/nd/	stand, round
/nt/	student, count
/sk/	scarf, skirt, basket, scary
/sm/	small
/sn/	snow
/sp/	sports, space
/st/	stand, first, stay
/sw/	swim, sweet
/tw/	twelve, twins
/kw/	quick, question

Three-Letter Consonant Blend

/spr/	spring
/str/	street
/skr/	screen
/skw/	square

Vowels

🇺🇸 /ɑː/ 🇬🇧 /ɒ/	top, jog, wash
/æ/	cat, clap, sand
/e/	wet, send, healthy
/ɪ/	hit, sing, pin
/ɔː/	caught, saw, cough
🇺🇸 /ɔːr/ 🇬🇧 /ɔː/	horse, morning
/eɪ/	cake, name, say
/iː/	eat, tree, steam
🇺🇸 /oʊ/ 🇬🇧 /əʊ/	home, coat, snow
/uː/	food, glue, flew, June
/ʌ/	duck, run, cut, honey
/ʊ/	cook, foot, put
🇺🇸 /ər/ 🇬🇧 /ə/	ruler, teacher
/ɜːr/	bird, hurt, word, learn

Diphthongs

/aɪ/	nice, bike
/aʊ/	house, brown
/ɔɪ/	boil, enjoy
🇺🇸 /aːr/ 🇬🇧 /aː/	card, market
🇺🇸 /aɪr/ 🇬🇧 /aɪə/	fire, hire
🇺🇸 /aʊr/, /aʊər/ 🇬🇧 /aʊər/	hour, flower
🇺🇸 /er/ 🇬🇧 /eə/	chair, bear, there
🇺🇸 /ɪr/ 🇬🇧 /ɪə/	near, engineer
/juː/	cute, huge, few

Vowel and Consonant Blend

/ʃən/	station, dictionary
/ɪz/	beaches, bridges
/ɪd/	visited

Contents

1 a e

🇬🇧 **British**
can
🇺🇸 **American**
soda can

1 🎧 02 Listen, point, and repeat.

 a

1

soda can

 e

2

Ken

3

man

4

men

5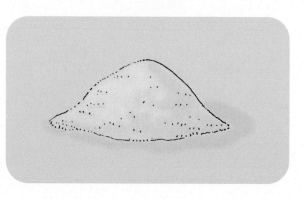

sand

6

send

2 🎧 💬 Listen and read.

1 This is a sandman.

2 His name is Ken.

3 Ken can have some friends.

4 Let's make some more sandmen.

3 ✏️ Draw another sandman. Give him a name.

1

e i

🇬🇧 **British**

bin
tin

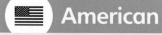
🇺🇸 **American**

trash can
tin can

4 🎧 04 Listen, point, and repeat.

e

1

Ben

2

bin

3

pen

4
pin

5

ten

6

tin

5 🎧 💬 Listen. Then say.

Ben put ten pens in the tin can.
Can Ben put ten pins in the trash can?

6 ⚙️ Count the pins, the pens, and the trash cans in your classroom.

2 o u

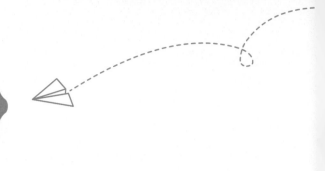

1 🎧 06 Listen, point, and repeat.

o

1

dog

3

jog

5

rob

u

2

duck

4

jug

6

rub

1

I took my dog on a jog.

2

My dog dug a hole in the mud.

3

I gave my muddy dog a bath.

4

I rubbed my dog with a towel.

3 **Act out the story.**

Review 1

1 08 🗨 **Listen and say the words.**

1

man
men

2

Ken
can

3

pin
pen

4

dig
dog

5

hat
hot

6

net
not

7

jog
jug

8

cap
cup

9

red
rub

e i o u

2 🗨 **Choose and write nine words. Play *Bingo*.**

1 _____

2 _____

3 _____

4 _____

5 _____

6 _____

7 _____

8 _____

9 _____

3 a_e

1 🎧 **Listen, point, and repeat.**

1 cage

2 page

3 cake

4 take

5 game

6 name

2  ♫ Listen. Then sing.

Take your cake and eat it.
Everybody do the same.
Take your cake and eat it.
That's the name of the game.

3 What's your favorite cake? Tell a partner.

3

i_e

1

nice

2

rice

3

bike

4

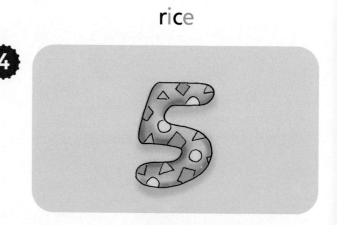

five

5

kite

6

side

Ride my bike
Up the side of a hill,
Ride my bike
Up the side of a hill.
Ride my bike
All over the place.
Please ride with me.

6 **Act out the song.**

4 o_e

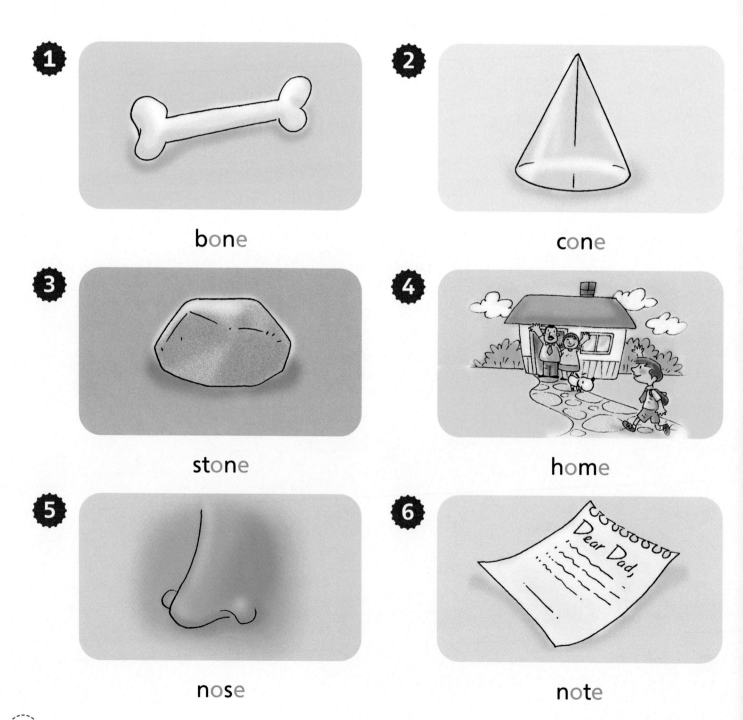

1 bone

2 cone

3 stone

4 home

5 nose

6 note

2 🎧 💬 Listen and read.

I have a lovely ice-cream cone.
The ice cream goes up my nose.

My dog has a lovely bone.
He buries it under a stone.

3 ⚙️ Act out the story.

4  u_e

4 🎧 **Listen, point, and repeat.**

1

cube

2

tube

3

cute

4

huge

5

tune

6

------ me, Miss.

excuse

5 Listen and read.

A huge friendly monster lives near me.
I hear him sing a cute tune.
"Excuse me, Monster, can I sing with you?
Can we sing tunes together?"

6 Make up a cute monster tune.

Review 2

a_e

1 🎧 💬 **Listen and say the words.**

1

Sam   same

2

Kit   kite

3

not   note

4

cut   cute

2 🎧20 Listen and write words in the correct places.

_a_	_a_e
_____	_____
_____	_____
_i_	**_i_e**
_____	_____
_____	_____
_o_	**_o_e**
_____	_____
_____	_____
_u_	**_u_e**
_____	_____
_____	_____

5 ea / ee

1 🎧 21 Listen, point, and repeat.

ea

ee

1

eat

2

tree

3

beach

4

week

5

sea

6

see

2  **Listen and read.**

I climb to the top of a tree.
I see as far as the sea!
I take some rice and tea.
I live for a week in a tree at the beach.

3 **What else can you take to the tree?**
Tell a partner.

5 **ar**

1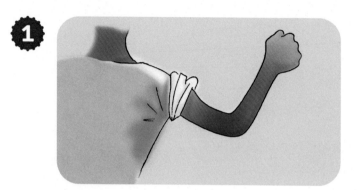

arm

2

farm

3

card

4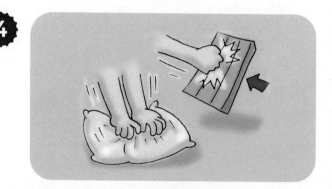

hard

5

tart

6

market

5 Listen and read.

I put a duck under my arm.

I put a tart on my head.

I go to the market. Why is everybody laughing?

6 Can you answer the question in the story?

6 or

1. horn

2. horse

3. fork

4. short

5. corner

6. morning

It is morning at the farm.
A baby horse is born.
He sits in the corner.
He says "Good morning" to all the horses.

3 ⚙ **Act out the story.**

Good morning!

6 er

British
clever
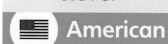
American
smart

4 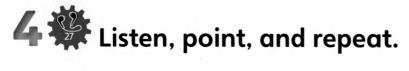 **Listen, point, and repeat.**

1

$$\sqrt{169} \times 754 = 9802$$

clev**er**

2

fath**er**

3

rul**er**

4

teach**er**

5

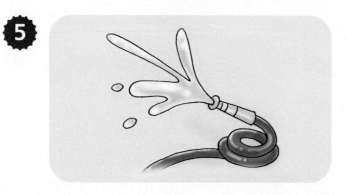

wat**er**

6

roll**er** coast**er**

5  **Listen. Then say.**

My teacher takes me on a roller coaster.
The roller coaster goes into the water.

6 **Do you like riding on the roller coaster?**
Tell a partner.

Review 3 ea / ee

1 Play the game. Say words with the sounds.

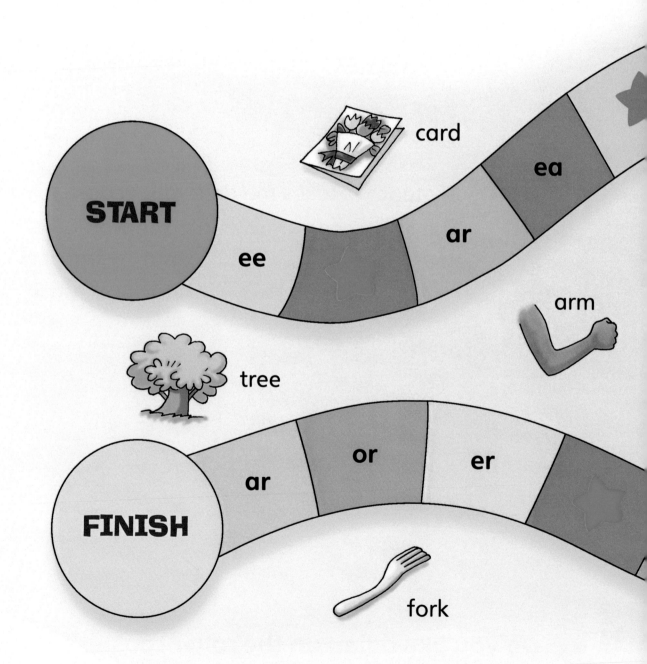

START

ee

card

ea

ar

arm

tree

or

er

ar

FINISH

fork

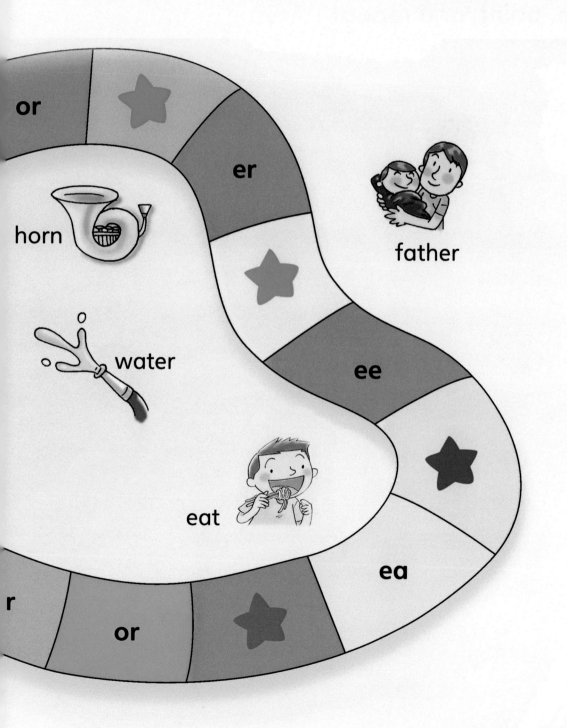

or

er

horn

water

father

ee

eat

ea

or

short **oo**

1  **Listen, point, and repeat.**

1

g**oo**d

2

w**oo**d

3

b**oo**k

4

c**oo**k

5

l**oo**k

6

f**oo**t

2  🎵 Listen. Then sing.

Take a look in a book.
Read a story or two.
It's good to learn about
Something new.
And I'm sure you'll find
You're glad that you
Took a look in a book.

3 Bring your favorite book to class. Tell a partner about it.

In my book …

7 long **oo**

4 🎧 32 **Listen, point, and repeat.**

1 boot

2 food

3 moon

4 noon

5 roof

6 school

I go to school on the moon.
The moon bus goes too fast.

We eat our food on the moon.
We wear moon boots to play ball.

On the moon ...

6 **Talk about life on the moon with a partner.**

8 ou / ow

1 🎧 34 Listen, point, and repeat.

 ou

ow

1

house

2
brown

3

loud

4

cow

5

mouse

6

now

2  Listen. Then say.

A little white mouse
Now lives in my house.
When I hear a loud shout,
It means mom found out.

3 Act out the chant.

8 oi / oy

4 🎧 36 💬 **Listen, point, and repeat.**

oi

1

b**oi**l

oy

2

b**oy**

3

YOUTH CLUB

j**oi**n

4

enj**oy**

5

c**oi**n

6

t**oy**

5  Listen. Then say.

1

> Quick! Let's boil some water. We can enjoy a cup of tea.

2

> The boys can play with their toys. We can all enjoy ourselves.

6 Act out the mothers and the boys.

8 ay

7 🎧 38 Listen, point, and repeat.

1
bay

2
day

3
May

4
pay

5
say

6
way

8  Listen. Then sing.

Can I stay all day and play?
Can I stay all day and play?
If I have my way,
If I have my way,
Can I stay all day and play?

9 Use you and your.
Sing another song.

Can you stay ... ?

Review 4

short & long
oo

1 🎧 41 💬 **Play the game. Say the names of the pictures or the rhyming words.**

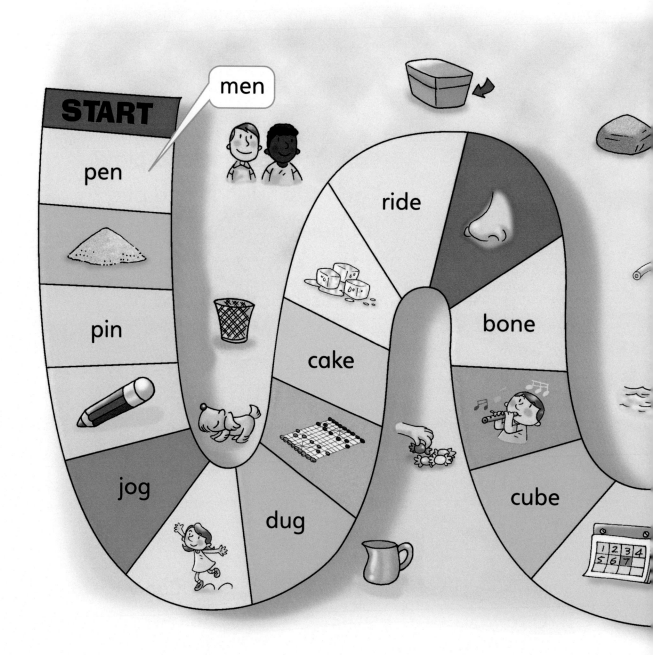

ou / ow oi / oy ay

more...

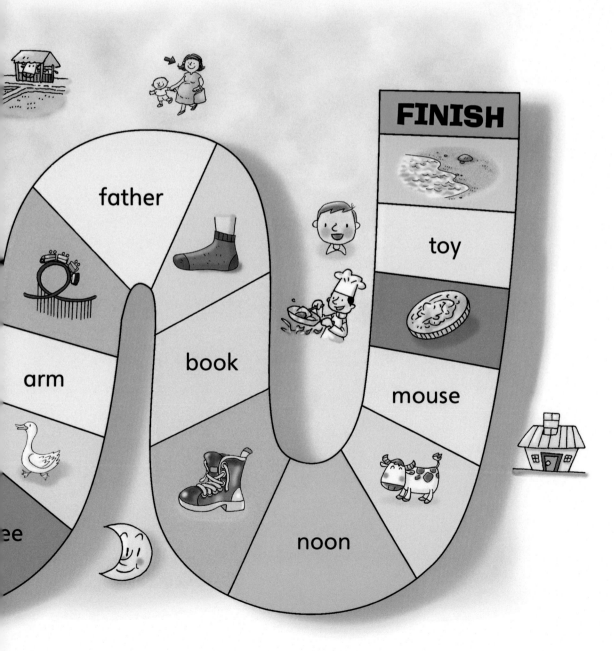

father

book

arm

noon

FINISH

toy

mouse

ee

PHONICS DICTIONARY

a / e

soda can	Ken	man	men	sand	send

e / i

Ben	bin	pen	pin	ten	tin

o / u

dog	duck	jog	jug	rob	rub

a_e

cage	page	cake	take	game	name

i_e	nice	rice	bike	five	kite	side
o_e	bone	cone	stone	home	nose	note
u_e	cube	tube	cute	huge	tune	excuse
ea ee	eat	tree	beach	week	sea	see

PHONICS DICTIONARY

 ar

arm	farm	card	hard	tart	market

 or

horn	horse	fork	short	corner	morning

 er

clever	father	ruler	teacher	water	roller coster

 short oo

good	wood	book	cook	look	foot

long oo	boot	food	moon	noon	roof	school
ou ow	house	brown	loud	cow	mouse	now
oi oy	boil	boy	join	enjoy	coin	toy
ay	bay	day	May	pay	say	way

Pearson Education Limited
KAO TWO
KAO Park
Hockham Way
Harlow, Essex
CM17 9SR
England
and Associated Companies throughout the world.

english.com/englishcode

Authorized Licenced Edition from the English language edition, entitled Phonics Fun, 1st edition
published Pearson Education Asia Limited, Hong Kong and Longman Asia ELT © 2003.

This Edition © Pearson Education Limited 2021

First published 2021

Fifth impression 2024

ISBN: 978-1-292-32257-5

Set in Heinemann Roman 17/19pt

Printed and bound by CPI Group (UK) Ltd, Croydon, CR0 4YY

Illustrated by Christos Skaltsas (Hyphen S.A.)